GW00633914

# CONSENT

## Kimberly Campanello

Doire Press

First published in March 2013


Doire Press
Aille, Inverin
Co. Galway
www.doirepress.com


Cover design & layout: Lisa Frank
Cover image: Tony Carragher
Author photo: Tony Carragher


Printed by Clódóirí CL
Casla, Co. na Gaillimhe

Copyright © Kimberly Campanello

ISBN 978-1-907682-23-0

All rights reserved. No part of this publication may be reproduced or transmitted in any form or by any means. This book is sold subject to the usual trade conditions.

# ACKNOWLEDGEMENTS

Acknowledgments are due to the editors of the following publications where some of these poems were first published: *Abridged, Burning Bush II, can-can, Eyewear, The Stinging Fly, Tears in the Fence* and *Upstart*. Wurm im apfel published the pamphlet *Spinning Cities* in 2011.

I wish to thank the following people for their ongoing support and encouragement: Joel Brouwer, Maggie Butt, Patrick Chapman, Mary Costello, Kit Fryatt, Dylan Griffith, Joanne Hayden, Brian Kavanagh, Gleny Köhnke, Dave Lordan, Declan Meade, Susan Melrose, Cheryl Moskowitz, Fran Quinn, Sean O'Reilly, Barra O Seaghdha, Todd Swift, Caroline Wynne, my parents Michelle and Fritz, and my brother Gregory.

Further thanks to the residency at Fundación Valparaíso in Mojácar, Spain, where I began writing this collection. Finally, thanks to Benjamin Dwyer, who ensures that there is never a dull moment.

# CONTENTS

*The assumption that spaces are autonomous has enabled the power of topography successfully to conceal the topography of power.*

— Akhil Gupta and James Ferguson

*... both force and consent enter into an achieved unity, a class alliance, marked by wounds of that process. (Isn't 'consent' simply another way of naming relations of force that have managed to secure certain willing conducts?)*

— Vinay Gidwani

# Consent

*A little Contra-Terrene matter among the pure shit of the poets —*
*The world's inescapable evil that we must eat and sing.*
                                                    — Thomas McGrath

Shit makes me
involuntarily hungry.
Shit or its wafting smell.
Rape makes me
involuntarily horny.
Rape or a scene of rape
(portrayed).
Consent is
physiological.
Involuntary sympathy
to voluntary movement.
Upon reflection,
agree not to resist
or prevent.
Acquiesce and permit.
Antonyms that bind consent.
My bowels are bound
on cheese and fear.
Meaning my shit is bound
for another bright white port.
A port can be entered
more or less freely.
We dock ships there
after all. We dock the tails
of certain dogs that agree
with coercion
not to resist becoming
the breed they were born.
We breed certain people
and bind them.

I bind you and you
like it all right.
We bind others—
bound to be a man
and a woman—
and say *let no man
put asunder*.
Man makes
voluntary movements
with guns
and involuntarily
puts others asunder.
This makes
some horny,
involuntarily.
Man makes
involuntary movements
with guns
and does the same,
voluntarily,
upon reflection.
This makes some
acquiesce.

# Little Haiti

*And the body lay born, beside the hacked off head.*　　— Ted Hughes


It's been a good day, I say, on 1st Ave., Little Haiti.
The goat was born easily and the moon
is wider than the widest high-rise
on the 41st Street beach where Orthodox
Jewish women powerwalk in covered
hair and long black sleeves and skirts.
The youngest child shrieks at the goat
in more Kréyol than English,
and the eldest grabs my camera
insists on taking picture after
picture until he gets the right one.
In the end it's blurry and I look happy
next to the pigs sleeping in the boat
with its hull torn out.
But we've made very little progress.

Or progress is a misnomer. Few of the neighbors
have doors and not because they have a different
definition of public and private.
I look to the placenta in the dust
and the bottle flies covering it.
Is there something to it? Clean and unclean.
The mother was supposed to eat it. The cord hangs
from the baby's gut, covered in its very first shit.
We all have to learn to shit neatly
and not roll around in it after.
Does this thought obscure the freshness
of the moment? Little David wants to know the date,
October 4th, and he sings *Happy Birthday*.
The people missing limbs who line the streets here
aren't fresh, but they are tidily placed

in memories of the Papa Doc days.
They aren't neat, but their stumps
end neatly. Someone shat on them
and walked away. Didn't roll around after.

## A Watermelon

A watermelon cracked open by an oily fist
flashes its guts in a truck bed.
A pregnant woman buys two of them
as elbows and knees poke her stomach from the inside.

# The Green

*D'aller là-bas vivre ensemble!*
*Aimer à loisir,*
*Aimer et mourir*
 *Au pays qui te ressemble!*                    — Charles Baudelaire

I'm bleeding out on the Green
and there are ass bandits standing by waiting for someone better
with a hole less unpredictable, less full of teeth and silent screams.
I am bleeding out on the Green waiting
for a whole human being to emerge. But it's too soon.
Maybe I am that human. Maybe you are half of it.
Maybe there's nothing even
about what we might make.
Maybe I'm making human being
seem too important.

Workers are tossing gold geraniums into a barrel
pulling them whole from the ground
and I keep seeing the same guy
wearing a dog collar everywhere I go. He has mud
on his velvet boots and he looks me in the eye
as if to say the mud is old mangos and the mud is old
hearts and the mud is old books that I gave away or let rot.

There is space and there
is space
I tell you.

And there is disgrace.

In Germany they scrub out
their trashcans.

Old nature didn't ask for this.
To be the receptacle of our fantasies. Old nature didn't say
pick me to be the woman
turned into a map and charted and uncharted
for the sake of what you think you don't know.
Her *mons pubis* is the treasureland and her breasts the entryway.
A good thing cartographers knew something about foreplay.

I am bleeding out on the Green
and the Green could be anywhere
suffused with whatever meaning I say.
Like the Green is Florida's sea grape trees
with roots that trip me up as horseshoe crabs
flee my heavy *Fleurs du mal* step
and old women toss grapes into a bowl to make
sea grape jelly to scrape onto crackers for schoolchildren
to make them see the land is important, to keep them from building
more high-rises and boating over more manatees
and refusing to turn out their lights that make turtle
hatchlings march toward Wal-Mart
instead of the sea.

Or the Green is Saint Stephen's in Dublin
where cops with long capes once shielded
men pissing straight liquor onto the grass
but never the women with blood on their thighs.
The best I could do is enter a pub
where the snug's walls have been taken down
now that women can be trusted to mingle
in the whole space and order their drinks at the bar
instead of through a little window with a sliding door.
But the snug is in my mind as they say.
A painful dialectic. The snug
is where you cut yourself down to half. Where you say no

to half, where you can say anything at all and it's
of no consequence. There is space and there is
space I say. A useful dialectic. The snug is where you go
to talk about bleeding out on the Green. The snug is where you go
and keep yourself on guard. The snug is only in my mind. It's not real.
Right. I can do anything, go anywhere
and no one will touch me. Least of all when I am bleeding
out on the Green. Least of all when I am the old woman
picking sea grapes. Least of all when I am helping nature refuse.
When I am taking this blood right out.
When I am taking out a whole human. Being. Or a half. My half.

Or the Green is generality. As though that's possible.
The *Generalife* gardens of the Alhambra
where the flowing water is louder
than my mind where the snug is still built
louder than the ping of sea grapes
in the metal bowl. Step onto the Green.
Bleed out. Breathe out. In.

# Eggshell Skull Rule

*Defendants must take their victims*
*as they find them.* Even still—
isn't it the boy's thin skull
that really causes his death? Or is it
the other boy's pummeling?

In my self-defense, as to your condition,
my own allows me to see
only a blank coin in your palm
and a block of wood at your feet
that could become a guitar for you to play.

I have no certainty about my condition
other than it precludes and requires unmarked roads,
ash from mountain fires and an old farmer
with his dominos joining me at the table saying—
*I just want to tell you,*
*I am a man and you are a woman.*
*But we are equal*
*in my mind.*

And how did I find you?
And you, me?
As is.

# Signs

*These fragments I have shored against my ruins.*      — T.S. Eliot

There are signs and it's not even April.
Isis hasn't begun to gather up the bloody bits
of her lover-son and the ceramic Stations of the Cross
are stationed in Afghanistan until further notice.
Your nails scratch my palm, which holds
the future in runes, maybe ruins
if I hand myself over to the signs, the ones
that tell me what fabric softener to buy,
that I'm fat and hairy, that my clothes are ugly
and that I'd better hurry and donate my eggs
for $10,000 because I have blue eyes
and a couple of masters degrees
and people just love that.

The stairwells of the shopping mall
are full of bullet holes and bedding.
I am eating cheese that is more plastic
than whey. People are dying of disease.
Fat babies are refused health insurance
and a boy is thrown out of school
for cutting his food with a knife.
Hunger. People are dying of war.
People are dying of despair.
People are getting thrown out of their homes.
People never had homes to begin with.
People are just plain dying.
To feed an alligator a Twinkie

is to sign its death warrant and your own
and Alhambra Circle is home
to an eponymous hotel in Coral Gables,
which has no coral or gables.

It works every which way:
take and combine two place names. Add an *ism*.
The British Museum near the Imperial Hotel
is full of British Imperialism.
There are love signs and death signs
and signs of the ends and the beginnings.
There are signs that God is everywhere—
including my fingers that know just what to do.
And God is in the Constitution, of course.

# The American People

The American people are
What the American people want is
Americans, yes, Americans say
The American people tell me time and
Your everyday American might wonder
Americans on Main Street have had it up to
What the American people are sick of
Options for everyday Americans are decreasingly
Americans bring up that very thing
Americans over here chime in
The American people understand
Most Americans know better
Your average American can't figure out
The American people find it increasingly
Everyday Americans want
Americans find this sort of thing
The American people are sick and
Those American people on Main Street
The American people believe more than anything that
Most Americans know nothing about
I've heard everyday Americans argue
Americans say give us
The American people find it hard
The American people are better off than
Americans are weighing the
The American people are telling me
Every day Americans wake up

# Grandma

I don't know if you noticed
but a cat has taken a bird
and left a struggle of feathers on the porch

You know me
You don't know me
You know me

You burn through the bottoms
of four coffee pots
You serve your grandchildren
raw sausages on Sundays
When you're hungry
you eat ice cream

You forgo shots of botulism in the face
to stop the twitching in your eye
You are still beautiful
Like a baby mouse
your bones and veins
breathe through your skin

You wear his sweater
with the sleeves pushed up
tuck fresh Kleenex
under the wristband
with discretion
You know him

Your eye twitches and hones
You don't know me
You know me
You don't know me

You know me
You me

Take me to the kitchen
Show me how to do this

# Halloween, South Beach

*…Thou hast left behind*
*Powers that will work for thee; air, earth, and skies;*
*There's not a breathing of the common wind*
*That will forget thee…*
                    — William Wordsworth, 'To Toussaint L'Ouverture'

They're wearing skull masks and bone coats and blood lipstick and hair suits. It's Halloween and the body is getting denied all over again as sexy pirate costumes make a mockery of revolution. I just want to watch the clouds flirt with the moon, think alone about the water cycle and how I get to drink Abe Lincoln's piss and this guy wants to talk New Age bullshit and Jesus, the primary metaphysician: *He walked on water. If I cut off my arm, I am still me. We are spiritual, not physical beings.* I zone out (or my spiritual being zones out) and I nod and nod. To waste breath on a counterargument implies that breath is valuable, hardly a spiritual notion in the primary metaphysical sense. To you and only you I will say this because it is important: that guy over there with the dreadlocks down to his ankles would be at a loss if they were cut away. Those tubes of hair and air and sweat have their own climate and weigh nearly as much as I do. They carry 10,000 nights of loneliness or fucking or living however he lives. And even though you and I have exchanged blood and hair and cum and silm, you can't just unzip me and climb in like I'm a Catholic schoolgirl outfit on the sale rack. And yet when you trimmed your beard I was so pissed off. I was all over that hair, clinging for dear life. Now we float together in some Dublin sewer. And fingernails—a vital *vodou* ingredient—I'm not under yours anymore, but I have made it onto your guitar strings. Tomorrow, *c'est la Toussaint*, All Saints' Day, *Día de los Muertos*, and candles and eternal flames are selling out and I won't be told Jesus was the primary metaphysician as we drink his blood and eat his flesh. Toussaint L'Ouverture didn't lead a slave revolt and beat Napoleon in a sexy pirate costume to free only the spirit.

Bodies were chained and owned. Bodies were sold. The common wind-and-water cycle. The clouds flirting with the moon. Eternal flames, everlasting ink.

# We Protect the Weak

We protect the weak and call it love or ethics.
For the safety of our students this door
must remain closed at all times. *Ani yalda tova. I am a good girl,*
I tell the Israeli jeweler who is impressed with my Hebrew.
An American nearby says, *Fuck Israel.* I offer, *I am a bad girl. Ani yalda raa.*

To dance is a kind of paralysis. Muscles contract
in a certain way and we call it beautiful.
The men on the beach made me think
they were dancing tango, but instead one
was helping the other will his feet to remember

walking. If I had withered hands and always gave you
your pen with my teeth would you think it beautiful?
For the continued safety of our money
these checkpoints must remain closed
at all times. For the quality of our progeny these legs

must remain closed at all times. These minds.
This mouth. This heart. Why don't you substitute
*your* for *these* and *this*? See how it feels. *Ani yalda raa.*
Feel that. Feel me feel you. Tell me I'm good
and bad. *Tova* and *Raa*. Let us be both.

# Graftonia

Dublin's rivers are cemented over
but always running

under houses and shops,
through old crypts.

Some of us women
have rivers of hair running

over our entire faces. We pay
to have long strings caress them

and tear them out.
I saw a whole face

done once in a chemist.
I saw no tears running,

just the woman's eyes cementing
themselves to my chin and cheeks.

# Potato Experiment

Children take the soft ones
Stab them with toothpicks
Suspend them in water
Watch them grow without soil
The eyes are poison to eat
The eyes are where it starts

# Again and Better

*Fail again. Fail Better.* — Samuel Beckett

Some therapists recommend scheduling fight time to keep it from spilling over into every interaction. It's about time I picked one with you because the couple over there screaming at each other reminds me of how much we need to accomplish, you and I. Should we fight about guns and whether we have a right to bear them? Or gum, which you've already told me you want to grab right out of my mouth. Let's fight about birds. Which ones are beautiful in your view? And what is beauty? The belted kingfisher, the painted bunting, or the scarlet ibis? None of the above. The carrion eaters, the kletoparasites, are truly brilliant, the most beautiful to us. So we agree. Damn. What about politics? Gender politics. Am I inherently better, or are you? Whose brain is bigger? Whose cock or cock-like object? Everybody's happy here! Whose gender does better at math? But we don't care about math. Oh, yeah. Who deserves more, is of more value? Well…Who needs to constantly apologize for this state of affairs? Who needs to change it? For fuck's sake. Let's stage a money or family fight. Who had a tougher childhood, or who learned the best values? Overdone. Like the meals we each will fucking burn. Or how about a time fight, those are the best. Or money-time fights. Even better. You're not following the script. Stage right, you enter. I'm doing dishes. We look at a pile of bills. I wipe my hands on a dishtowel. You adjust your enormous cock. Oh, Stanley Kowalski. What time is yours, and only yours? And mine? Ours? Let's parry over milliseconds. Let's get out two metronomes and see whose life moves faster. Can we set a third on *Allegro ma non troppo*? No. Of course not. Please, let's fight about laughter, about when it's appropriate and when it's insulting. Let's insult each other. And laugh about it. Tell me again that you'd beat me before you'd fall out with me. A disturbingly beautiful sentiment. Let's buy an extra set of dishes just for breaking. An extra three sets. Please disappear for a week and then show up with hat in hand. I can't wait to smack you.

Let's block that scene now. Pay attention this time. A pit orchestra is here and the conductor neither of us likes. A musical? We hate them. The tempo? A *scherzo*?! Prop issue, script problem! We're both smacking each other with hats, laughing.

# 22<sup>nd</sup> Street, Miami Beach

*Complacencies of the peignoir, and late*
*Coffee and oranges in a sunny chair,*
*And the green freedom of a cockatoo...* — Wallace Stevens

On this Sunday morning the huddled masses are right here
under the oak trees sleeping it off on plastic bag pillows
as I eat it off with a $12 slice of pizza and a $6 beer.

This man on the curb has gout so bad I'm afraid
he can't move to a cooler spot when the Miami sun
rises high and the body builders start up their midday jogs.

Elsewhere, a census worker is lynched in Kentucky
and proposing health care makes you a Nazi.
When will we sleep this off and wake up somewhere else?

Let's thank god for public beach showers where each morning
the people lather up. Let's thank god the old woman hit by the cab
still has the strength to stand up and kick the door.

Let's thank god it's avocado season and they drop free
from the trees. There are so many they will rot.

# Status Update

I want to know
if these are sweatshop poems.
I want to know whose blood
is on my keyboard.

# Joanie's Blue Crab Shack

Maybe if we'd met when you were 30 and I was 15 you'd have ended up in prison and have worked each day scrubbing historic bricks to be re-laid in some pre-planned quaint downtown where people sip lattes and think about nice sweaters and movie star sex between people aged 15 years apart or more. I'd be forever 15 waiting for you in Ochopee, Florida, at Joanie's Blue Crab Shack where Raiford the country singer is frustrated with this table of Everglades tourists from Connecticut and the blackboard at the entrance warns: *If you want fast food, keep traveling 42 miles west or 66 miles east.* When the bikers come in, Raiford starts up a chat, breathes relief and better singing into the mic, asks if they know Alabama's Bar in Fort Lauderdale, *The kind of place you might walk into and see a knife fight.* To me, he throws a worried look. I appear to be 15 and already I've had four union-made PBRs this Sunday afternoon. Raiford calls himself the *Human Jukebox,* cycles through more cover songs, repeats to the J-Crew crew from Connecticut: *The kind of place you might walk into and see a knife fight. I do find that quite quaint, I do.* And maybe I'd join Raiford onstage and pick up the refrain: *I shot a man in Reno, just to watch him die./I built a Panera and a Starbucks, just to watch you die.* And maybe the people from Connecticut aren't so bad. They'd laugh and know that they themselves didn't actually build those chains, and we'd all laugh because each of us has eaten at one in a pinch. Maybe I'd wave goodbye and hop on one of those hogs and ride to Miami's I-195 causeway where you'd be living homeless in a tent city with other sex offenders now that you've been released and there are ordinances about how many miles must separate all of you from a school or a park because in Miami we're tripping over them (though the schools lack books and our parks have busted swings). And maybe on this back-bay bridge where coconut palms offer some shade and one of you has jammed an American flag into the ground I'd pull you from your tent and we'd sing loud over the generators powering tiny fridges *Just to watch this die, just to watch this die.*

# The Maya

The Maya get arrested on South Beach
for sitting on a bench for too many days.
They're patted down, hands behind head,
as though their pockets contain nuclear waste
and their backpacks are iPhones of destruction
with apps that could drain our bank accounts,
steal our women, and leave dog shit unscooped.
Even the rich man watching feels bad, tells me
they didn't have anywhere else to go.

That night I am walking alone, drunk
on a mix of five countries' beers.
It's another night when just my presence
is a come hither, when my cunt
seems to be tattooed on my face.
I see the empty bench and I'm scared.
There are no Maya to watch over me
as though they had special powers,
as though I was important.

I do realize that I'm romanticizing the Maya
and myself and that one day I will walk the streets
invisible, my old skin hanging from my bones
like money bags and the most anyone
will want from me is my wallet.
I hope that same day the Maya
will be people, not just an image in a poem
whose arrest signals the end of civilization
or the rape of a rich white girl.

# Saw Grass

The swamp deer eat
the sweet white tip
just before the root
where the serration stops.

# The Squatters

The squatters keep building tin houses
on my friend's land and he offers me
half its value if I go to Brazil with a machete
and some Portuguese and make them stop
for the next three years.
The squatters keep giving birth
without c-sections and use gravity
rather than forceps to let it all out.
The squatters keep breathing
in and out, in and out, *Sat Nam*.
*Truth is our highest identity.*
I am squatting over you, here, on the bed,
and godammit, I have to put *cunt*
in a poem one more time
because you are looking up at mine
saying, *Jesus*. To squat is to live free.
To squat is to trust that your insides
will get ripped out
in the best way possible.
To squat is to sink low at the knees,
but not lock them. To squat is to linger
and let the lips separate and speak
saying, *I can't imagine*
*never having known you.*

# At the Oktoberfest

At the Oktoberfest in Cape Coral she shows me
the ultrasound of her fetus that's well past the fish stage.
The eyes are open in the water. There's even a smile.

Here on the outside, blue herons are poking
at something, maybe fish, in a ditch
full of gasoline run-off and McDonald's bags.

It's noon and down the road on the Miccosukee reservation,
a man leans a sign against his fence as he does each day, even after
Obama. *George Bush we don't like your war. Go back to England.*

Here, the herons' greasy feathers hang and flap
from their bones like the fringe of this festive tablecloth.
The corner of the ultrasound image is slid

under a beer stein to keep it from blowing away.
Will I say that I want us all to go back to England,
or Germany, or wherever, with my eyes wide open, smiling?

Will I so ruin this celebration of impending birth and Germanness?
Will I say I am glad for this Saturday of out-of-tune waltzes
and sausages full of by-products?  Glad to stare

the next generation in the viscous, beer-stained face?
I can only say that I am not smiling. My eyes are open.
I am thrilled not to be in that water.

# Christmas Eve, Rathmines

Woolen tights over basically bones,
her dragged shopping frame
sturdier than those.
The sack's skin flapping
over what must be
milk, please a small ham,
let's also say an orange.

# A Man

A man holds out his lack-of-hand
with its screw-in porcelain cup and asks for change.
The child dressed like a *puta* tells me
to fuck off with her kohled eyes.

# Caged Bird

Once we've soaked it in wine and melted butter,
we wonder if this bird will fit in our oven
or if the whole thing will explode.
And its origin? Is it free-range or wild?
What if it lived in a fenced field but no one fed it?
Or if its mother threw herself in front of a car
without knowing what a car was?
Our sacrificial bird of unknown origin does
fit in the oven. Its skin gets nice and crispy
as its gizzard boils down in a dented pot for gravy
while its head lolls in the gut wagon miles away
from this rented cabin in southern Indiana
where we've come to spend Thanksgiving.
We've parked our Lexus SUV
and brought in crates of foreign beers
and fine wine to mull along with our beliefs
about meat, abortion, war.
A beer from Czechoslovakia softly buzzes us
and we discuss our desire not to die and how that
makes us human. Or is it our desire to die?
What of our special knowledge of death's meaning?
A caged bird can hang itself if it wishes.
Nevertheless, a caged bird sings.
A beer from Belgium hammers us.
Fractals of birch and maple slice
a blacker black into the black sky.
Nearby a father tucks his children into bed
with tales of black rapists and devil Catholics
and the story of AIDS, God's cure for homosexuality.
We really should buy this wine from Chile again.
In the yard an oak tree is tied up
with faded yellow ribbon not strong enough
to stunt the growth that will soon shred it
though the troops won't be even close to home.

Fractals of birch and maple slice
a blacker black into the black sky.
The turkey's head in the gut wagon.
The fetal cranium in the canula.
The boy's head that ends in bomb.
A caged bird can hang itself, does. A caged bird sings.

# Sunday Morning

The seeds of the royal palm look like puke
or flax. Up in the fronds bees are knocking them
around and down onto the pavement.
On the corner a couple in wheelchairs sing—
*This summer I hear the drumming, four dead in Ohio.*
Down further a guy hoses the sidewalk
toward sewer grates that filter out used condoms,
fake eyelashes, handbills, actual retch.
Some of the spray hits my ankle.
Whatever doesn't wash down will dry out
in the Miami sun and be swept into a dustpan.

This is the point in the poem where I must sing such beauty.
The world—its complexities and contradictions.
And I hesitate.

Yesterday at the nude beach I paid six dollars
to take off all my clothes and roast my ass
to match my back. I stretched out
on the border between the gay section and the rest.
My head pointed toward bears and leather daddies.
My arms reached toward the small island of lesbians.
My ankles were nearly in with the straights.
I thought I could feel them preparing
to yank me over by the Achilles tendons.
I fell asleep wondering if my labia
are visible if I'm flat on my stomach
with my legs together. They are
pretty long. I thought I felt a bug
crawl between my legs
but it was just sweat trickling,
and when I sat up, there it was,
the test of my poet's vision:
the longest, sweatiest foreskin I have ever seen

pink and glistening in the sun like folded, sliced ham.
The French call my feeling *le dégoût*. Disgust.
The stronger adjective is *dégueulasse*. Revolting.
It wasn't any other body there that day
or any other body part that caused it.
And there were all sorts.
And now at this café these people next to me
are eating a pizza with that guy's foreskin
spread all over it. I ask them
if the pizza is good. *Yes, it really is.*
I reach into my bag where the powder waits.
I tear it from the package that says,
*classic beige*, *lightweight*, and *natural*.
I spread it on my sweating, porcine face.

# Three Boys

Three boys in identical shirts
dance in the square
where the church wall still says
José Antonio Primo de Rivera.
In death slang, they call the host,
the body of Christ, a whore.
They promise to shit
in the skulls of our dead ancestors.

# Bar Oliver, Granada

The muck-colored fish called *rapé*
stretches her bulk across the ice. She rages
with yellow teeth and saggy jowls.

No one has asked for her today.
Sleeker fish are plucked
from above by clean hands,

dragged through breadcrumbs, fried.
A boy and girl examine the *rapé*,
tap the glass, try to wake her.

Tomorrow she will be ordered up unknowingly
as the soup stock where fresher fish float.
The singer wheels her music-maker

into the square and announces herself.
No one asked for her and her short shirt
revealing loose flesh. No one asked

for her orange flip flops that come free
with pedicures in America.
No one ordered. No one asked.

She sweats through her clothes.
Her face is cold and dry.
Her face is like the ice

crowned with the *rapé*.
Her face is like the dust
where the dead are piled and arranged.

She closes her eyes during the intro
to *Spanish Eyes. Dammit*, you say,
*she's good.* But no one has ordered her.

No one asked. She is not required
in this moment. She sings.
A plate is handed through the open window.

A mass grave of golden *boquerones* gleaming
in the sun. You explain a tiny fish
you once had in Málaga, how it must be ordered illegally,

how the meat is so beautiful and sweet,
how the population won't replenish
if they are taken so young.

# In the Hills

In the hills of Víznar, British Petroleum has set up shop
where Lorca and thousands of others were shot.

In the hills of Níjar, the legs of the dead goat
slung under the tree have landed in a trot.

# Childhood Clothes

I.

Nuns sewing clothes in Granada
for baby Jesus dolls
for their whole lives
for as long
as anyone can remember
trunkfuls of velvet and lace and burlap and linen
Christ baby as judge
Christ baby as king
Christ baby as shepherd
Christ baby as child

Yet in a book on the history
of Spanish photography
there's a shot of a little girl
just 50 miles away
from this same convent
with no pants on
only a tiny sweater
around her shoulders
her hairless lips
swelling before my eyes
She looks down
at her clapping hands
as the children
play flamenco dancer and *palmeros*
in front of the *Torre del Oro*

II.

There are dangerous games
that should be played
and I got to play them
riding bareback
into a flooded field
in a thunderstorm
my bare feet dragging
through run-off
electrical towers all around
lightning
an animal that can kill
sweet risk
and afterwards
fresh clothes
a soft towel
to dry off with

# On Red Arrow Highway

On Red Arrow Highway
the cat's leg is *rigor mortised* in a salute.
Children scramble on hands and knees
in the cemetery, chasing hot shells
that rain down from 21 guns.
The US Army chaplain holds a feather
and a knife wrapped in beaded leather.
He explains Memorial Day and the role
of warriors in his tribe and in America.
He prays to the Earth, the Great Spirit, and Jesus Christ.

That night at the table my father says,
*They lost. The Indians. They should have*
*fought harder. They should quit whining.*
I am holding a bone to my mouth.
I am licking and biting and sucking.
I am tossing it into a bowl with the others.
I could counter with a list of fighting things—
drones, democratically-elected leaders deposed
and replaced by dictators, assisted
ethnic cleansing, Fort Benning,
the Glocks we buy for our kids
to shoot on the ranges or at school.

We sit and chew ribs with salt and beer.
We separate spine from flesh.
We talk with bones in our mouths.
We talk with our mouths full of them
and what we say is dead and hollow.

# Chicken Skin

When you don't bread a chicken body
you see its skin quite clearly.
Feather hairs once emerged from raised holes.
And some people plan
rape fantasies just to feel
their arms and legs
spread at the sockets
like the chicken's legs and wings
before they're cut from the body.
And maybe that makes some sense.
This is not a vegetarian poem
but you should know
that there's no real fixity—
the uterus and fallopian tubes
just float inside us.
I never really saw chicken skin
until at 18 I saw the inside
of my *labia majora*.
I had worried it was wrong.
I was wrong. The nurse said
*No, that's your chicken skin.*
*We all have it. Just ask any of us.*

# Out of the Cradle

*From the thousand responses of my heart, never to cease.*
— Walt Whitman

I note the wreck of bodies all around me—ridges of cellulite
on thin thighs, breast implants gone astray, puffy wrists
and elbows, permanent brow furrows, the right soft hair
in all the wrong places, hair that's missing.
In the sea, I cup a jellyfish in each palm and think of breasts,
how on women and men they are rocks to grab onto
as the sea tries to drag you out.

My friend told me once that he loved my skin,
that it expressed my freshness, my full heart.
But it's changing each day in this brutal sun
as I sit with my favorite books, freeing the poet, crossing off
lines of her poems so instead of begging him not to leave
she ends with, *I am alone. I must discover my heart/against rock.*

At the Playa de la Piedra Villazar we square-danced in the water,
and I scraped my ankle on submerged rock. My skin,
my heart, against rock. Not being alone, I didn't really notice.
Did you notice the way I grabbed your chest
when we faced each other last? *Piel, corazón, piedra.*
I am alone. I must cross off something. Free
someone. Note the wreck of my body rocked.

# Lewisham Hospital

We meet the sick, piled and waiting
on beds and wheelchairs.  Above us,
the *Madonna del Parto* opens her tunic
to just a slit, casually displays
her pregnant stomach. The angels
pull back the curtains to reveal her:
the human vulva. Smug and fecund,
she interferes with the rattling lungs,
the pale, hairless children, and this man
eating a crisp off the floor.

You are *11 a.m. testes*. We sit and wait.
A Rothko looms blood black, an open square,
an exit needing entry, framed in pine and screwed
into the wall above the water fountain
where a girl flattens a whole stack
of paper cups in a bear hug and puts them back
in their corner. We are called.

The nurses pull back the curtains
to reveal her, the doctor in her *hijab*
who casually tells you where
to put your penis. She pulls back
the curtains of your scrotum with her probe
and some gel, reveals images of sound.
We search for echoes on the screen.

The right teste hugs itself
in its dark cave, disperses
with the probe's plain music.
I try to remember anatomy.
Where are we now? Epididymis.
The granary, the dark tunnel
where the seed gets stored. Dark and quiet

like the silo I was told not to play in.
The grain bearing down, filling lungs,
our corpses discovered only in late winter
when last year's seed has nearly run out.
Suddenly the left teste shouts
its egg shape, its pure boundaries
and clear purpose. The white whale's back
emerges from the darkness,
interfering with the vulnerability
we are here to investigate.

# Cut and Pressed

*...the fascism in us all, in our heads and in our everyday behavior, the fascism that causes us to love power, to desire the very thing that dominates and exploits us.* — Michel Foucault

I.

She says he pressed the pads of her fingers
to see if they came back pink. He checked
her pussy lips against the pale plastic rose
he bought her at the gas station.
He pronounced her white, said he never
could have imagined as a child in Jamaica that he
would have such a pure woman. He grabbed
her hair, wrapped it around his arm
like a golden butler's towel on his tuxedo skin.

*You see*, she tells me, *in this fucked-up world
you and I are benefiting from hundreds of years
of racism. You see, we have blue eyes.*
She shows me the picture in her phone
of him reading Foucault, his head leaning
against a red and yellow Care Bear pillow.
I tell her no man believes me when I lie
and say I'm from Miami. You look
like you're from the North, they say. And north
means white. And north means not Jewish.
She tells me he refers to himself as a mongrel.

II.

I wonder what you saw in the Braille of my skin
in the darkness of that first night
when your white Irish fingers traced my white American folds?
Are there racial messages between us
or is it the pure love-making
only white on white can have?
This            makes            no      sense.
        And who        is watching this unfold
from the panopticon?

There were signs: *No dogs or Irish.*
My grandfather from Bari was read
as black.

Whoever the census lists separately.
        Batteries of munitions sold separately.
Your cock shudders inside me.
                The shuttles of looms
that cut off countless fingers.
Five points of light flash
                in my eyelids
resurrecting the Five Points slum
                                where the Irish
and emancipated slaves        mingled.
I want to believe we are redeeming
                                something and enough fingers
                have been cut and lips pressed.

# April, Dublin

Spring hangs leaves indiscriminately,
throws down dandelions onto vacant lots.
Another body is loosened from the canal bottom
by a cormorant gulping fresh spawn.
Councils purge piebald horses,
round them up for secret executions
as families tidy Tidy Town hopefuls,
blow dust from the paths
though it blows back in their faces,
blast moss from the stone wall at the crossroads
where the boy made his gallows speech
for stealing an apple
before he was hanged and wrapped
in the freshest sheet his skin had ever touched.
In these long-lit days women walk home
a different way, or a little later
or in less clothing.
Some regret it. Others know they could.
That old phrase of possession
meant as a deterrent—
*Would you want someone to do that*
*to your own sister?*
*Imagine she is your daughter.*
Though in that speech the boy said it—
*The apple was not mine—*
and was hanged anyway.
In my kitchen I get down
on hands and knees
and scrub floors the Alabama way
and think of kettlefuls
of boiling water poured down
women's throats by priests
or members of the laity
and how some folks pressure-hosed

some others or hanged them
from live oak trees.

# A Black-faced Bird

A black-faced bird sits down at the table,
gives out hell to me, says to throw away
the funeral parlor advertisements
attached to the flowers clutched by the dead.

# Now

I.

Now the wracked bodies
of charred rabbits
have disappeared
from the fields
and the village is flooded
with people who can't
speak the language.
Each day we help each other
peel back our eyelids
despite the sun.
We prepare food
with a rusting knife
made by a child
we don't know
laboring
on the other side of the world.
We sharpen
a hundred pencils each
and work on new lines
to press into our palms
new veins to line our legs
new omniscience
to goad our hearts.

## II.

To displace
the obelisk's
stacked stone
To invent new trumpets
tubas saxophones
To march
To attack first with rosemary
then predictions
to demand money
to accept tears
To run up the street
from our offices
in high heels
to grab our babies
to feed them
from our breasts
then and there
To light candles
in the grotto
to light so many
it will explode

III.

I squat over these rising white ribbons,
these maggots reaching
and twisting themselves

from a rotting leg joint.
They promise me
there are salves

for all of this.
Salves stronger
than nuclear waste

with a smell
that could fill a church
like incense.

Biologists say
a maggot's whole body
is covered with ocular cells,

eyes that never blink.
They always
respond to the light.

# Orange on the Horizon

*Comme le feu, l'amour n'établit sa clarté*
*que sur la faute et la beauté des bois en cendres...* — Philippe Jaccottet

Orange on the horizon—a boat with curved Viking sails
in flames. No, it's the moon rising. I still want to cry for help.
The ring-necked dove crying for help. The one with the broken

wing that we took to the rehabilitation center. *The only thing*
*to do with a ring-necked dove is wring its neck.* A non-native species,
they probably fed it to an ailing osprey. A boat with curved Viking

sails in flames. In Dublin, they built an office on the best
Viking site they had. *The only thing to do with a ring-necked*
*dove is wring its neck.* We're just mixed-up capitalists. It's nothing personal.

A fire—orange on the horizon—takes seven days to reach us.
Day one we laughed and skimmed ash off the sea. Day seven
the gardener stayed behind, drawing circles of water

around the horse, letting the cars finally explode.
Orange on the horizon—the surplus value we'll never extract.
I can't seem to drive my feet deep enough in the sand to hold me, to keep me

from treading water. I must float or stand. The moonrise
reproducing the means of production. This shoe is heavy and seeks
non-native species—Cuban tree frogs and iguanas—for smashing.

*The only thing to do with a ring-necked dove is wring its neck.*
Dear Orange on the Horizon, or to Whom It May
Concern: For just five minutes give us something different.

A tall glass building, windows with no drapery, and people
and doves we can watch rehabilitate. Draw a ring of ash
around my neck, for love. I will float and stand.

# Still

He told me how in his childhood
vultures used to mean a rush out to the hay fields
to see what had died. The worst was when his father

mowed over the fawn. A fawn is taught, or maybe just knows,
to hold still in danger. This is usually for the best.
If I hold still, is it for the best? If I hold still, how will you come?

The fawn held still. The mower tore it to pieces.
The vultures came and with them, the children. The father wept.
The hay was baled to feed the cows for slaughter.

I rushed on my bike to the tower through spinning cities of gnats.
We met, and they died all over me, my face and arms speckled with black.
Not one was still. No one is still. Ever. Not me. Not you. Even

the fawn breathed. I am building this spinning city
in a hay field. You are rushing to its tower.
We will meet there, breathing, still.

# Sanctus

*And what is death...your mother's or yours or my own?*

— James Joyce

I.

At the English pub in Indianapolis, we discuss technology. He says he can already hear the robot's footsteps on his grave. In the worst neighborhoods, the prairie is coming back. Cattails are pushing up through old sidewalks and nearly all the important species of sparrows have returned. A Future Farmer of America— in other words, a 14-year-old white kid from the pesticide-drenched heartland—slips backwards from a mall railing and falls to his death among the Super Pretzels and Dippin' Dots down in the food court. I get reminded of incest dreams and the two I've had, one for each parent. My mother calls and gives me the run-down on which of her friends is on a morphine drip and which is in remission, and she tells me that when I get back to Miami I should get a job and always keep a full tank of gas. The homilitic style of evangelical Christianity is the same in Ghana, San Diego, Little Havana, and on Ellettsville, Indiana's Hart Strait Road where in the abortion scene of the Halloween morality play she yanks a skinned squirrel soaked in beet juice from the screaming girl's crotch and holds it up with food-service tongs before tossing it on a cookie sheet. *You'll have a clean slate if you accept Jesus, right now. We'll all have a clean slate, if you accept Jesus, now.* The body of Christ. Amen. The body of Christ. Amen. The body of Christ. Amen. Don't drop it. Use a metal plate with a handle that could guillotine a communicant's neck. And on the third day, I drank *poitín* at an Irish pub in Bloomington, Indiana, in fulfillment of the scriptures. Take this, all of you, and drink it. This is the bloodshine of the newest and most everlasting covenant. Don't drop it.

II.

Death is a real bummer. We live through and for our parents
and still Freud was wrong. You should hurry up and put your
face right in it for an hour and that is definitely a sacrament,
more so than that night in Garrucha at the *misa flamenca*, though
the music was nice. Even the *Sanctus* didn't offend me. Finally,
I would add that the world is falling apart, always has been, *ubi
sunt qui ante nos fuerent*, etc., and that my favorite sounds are
when you say things like, *Everything is fine*, or, *That cunt is mine*.
I hear them and I clench and unclench and I. love. you.

Tell me it's too much. Amen.
Tell me it's too much. Amen.
Tell me it's too much. Amen.

Let us kneel down facing each other, holding razors.
Lather up my head and I will lather yours.
I am worthy to receive you.
I am your mirror. On which a razor
lay crossed. We'll shave it all off.
If our knees can handle it, let's stay like this
until it grows back, softer than before.
If they can't, let's make love, and say,
*These are our bodies,*
*which will not be given up*
*for any of you.*
Let us say our own word
and we shall be healed.

# NOTES

James Ferguson and Akhil Gupta's epigraph is taken from *Culture, Power, Place: Explorations in Critical Anthropology* (1997).

Vinay Gidwani's epigraph is taken from *Capital Interrupted: Agrarian Development and the Politics of Work in India* (2008).

p. 9     **Thomas McGrath**'s epigraph is taken from *Letter to an Imaginary Friend* (1997). **Contra-Terrene matter** is anti-matter, which is made up of anti-protons, anti-neutrons, and anti-electrons.

p. 11    The epigraph is taken from **Ted Hughes**'s poem 'February 17th' from *Moortown Diary* (1979). The **Little Haiti** neighborhood is home to Miami's Haitian community.

p. 14-16 The epigraph from **Baudelaire**'s 'L'Invitation au voyage' in *Les Fleurs du mal* (1854) translates to: 'To go there to live together/To love at our leisure/To love and to die/In the country that resembles you.' **Snugs** are enclosed sections or cubbies found in many Irish pubs. Up until the 1970's women were largely restricted to drinking in snugs (or were not admitted into pubs at all).

p. 17    A legal doctrine called the 'eggshell skull rule' holds a person liable for injury or death even if the victim is already in a vulnerable condition. According to Lord Justice Lawton (1975), a defendant *'must take their victims as they find them'*.

p. 18    The epigraph is taken from **T.S. Eliot**'s poem 'The Waste Land' (1922).

p. 23    Robert Hass resurrected the Anglo-Saxon word for female ejaculate— **silm**—in his poem 'Etymology' from *Time and Materials: Poems 1997-2005* (2007): 'And what to say of her wetness? The Anglo-Saxons/Had a name for it. They called it silm./They were navigators. It was also/Their word for the look of   moonlight on the sea'.

p. 28    The **Samuel Beckett** epigraph is from *Worstward Ho* (1983). ***Allegro ma non troppo*** and ***scherzo*** are musical tempo markings (in Italian) meaning 'fast but not too fast' and a 'fast, humorous section or work', respectively.

p. 30    The epigraph is from **Wallace Stevens**'s poem 'Sunday Morning' from *Harmonium* (1923). In 2009, a **US census worker** was lynched and had the word 'FED' scrawled across his chest. That same year US President Barack Obama was accused of being a **Nazi** due to his support of government funding for health care.

p. 32    A **PBR** is a Pabst Blue Ribbon, an American lager beer. **J-Crew** is a retail clothing company in the US. Due to sexual-predator laws in Miami requiring that **sex offenders** live no closer than 2500 feet to schools, daycares, libraries, and shopping centers, as well as several other types of public and private facilities that serve children, by 2009 roughly 60 sex offenders had settled on the **I-195** causeway (Julia Tuttle Causeway) that links the city of Miami on mainland Florida to the island of Miami Beach.

p. 34    Saw grass, the type of **grass** found in the Everglades of Florida (the reason for which the area is dubbed 'The Sea of Grass') is sharply serrated until just before it meets the earth.

p. 35    *Sat Nam* is a Sanskrit phrase variably translated to mean 'truth', 'truth is my identity', or 'true name [of God]'.

p. 36    Members of the **Miccosukee tribe** reside in south Florida on reservations on the Tamiami Trail (US-41) and Alligator Alley (I-75).

p. 37    Rathmines is an area in South Dublin.

p. 38    *Puta* is Spanish for 'prostitute'.

p. 43    **José Antonio Primo de Rivera** (1903-1936) was one of the founders of the Fascist Falange in Spain. Killed during the Spanish Civil War, he was upheld as a martyr by Franco in order to consolidate his support among Falangists, even though he was likely relieved by Rivera's death as it opened the way for his own dictatorship.

p. 44-45 *Boquerones* means 'sardines' in Spanish, and the word is used colloquially to refer to people from Málaga.

p. 47    *Palmeros* are musicians that provide the clapping in flamenco music. The *Torre del Oro* (which translates to 'tower of gold') is a 13th-century military watchtower in Sevilla, Spain.

p. 49      A **Glock** is a type of handgun.

p. 51      The epigraph is taken from **Walt Whitman**'s 'Out of the Cradle
           Endlessly Rocking' from *Leaves of Grass* (1860). The poet referred to
           is **Linda Gregg** and the **lines** that are left behind are taken from her
           collection *Chosen by the Lion* (1995). **Piel, corazón, piedra** translates
           from Spanish to: 'skin, heart, rock'.

p. 54      The epigraph from **Michel Foucault** is taken from his introduction to
           volume one of Deleuze and Guattari's book *Anti-Oedipus: Capitalism
           and Schizophrenia* (1972). The **panopticon** was invented by the 18th-
           century English philosopher Jeremy Betham. It is a building designed
           to act as an all-seeing eye—its structure is often used in correctional
           and mental health institutions. The word was famously used by
           Foucault as a metonym for power's regulatory saturation of daily life.

p. 62      The epigraph from **Philippe Jaccottet**'s poem 'L'Ignorant' from
           *L'Ignorant* (1958) is translated by Derek Mahon as: 'Love, like fire,
           can only reveal its brightness/on the failure and beauty of burnt
           wood.' Infestations by **non-native** 'invasive' species are increasingly
           common worldwide. Two such species in Florida are the **ring-necked
           dove** and the **Cuban tree frog**, which disturb the native ecosystem.

p. 64-65   The epigraph is from **James Joyce**'s *Ulysses* (1922). A *misa flamenca*
           is a Mass set to flamenco music. *'Ubi sunt qui ante nos fuerent'*
           translates from the Latin to: 'Where are those who went before us?'
           This sense of degradation and the idea that all that is great has already
           passed was a common trope used by medieval poets.

**KIMBERLY CAMPANELLO** was born in Elkhart, Indiana, and now divides her time between Dublin and London. Her pamphlet *Spinning Cities* was published by Wurm Press in 2011. She was featured poet in the Summer 2010 issue of *The Stinging Fly*, and her poems have appeared in magazines in the USA, Canada, the UK, and Ireland, including *Abridged*, *The Cream City Review*, *filling station*, *Irish Left Review*, *nthposition*, *Tears in the Fence*, and *The Penny Dreadful*. In 2011, she was selected to read as part of the Poetry Ireland Introductions Series. Kimberly has taught Creative Writing at Florida Gulf Coast University, Big Smoke Writing Factory (Dublin), Middlesex University (London), and the Irish Writers' Centre.

For more information please see: www.kimberlycampanello.com